MW00713227

The Redbud Tree

紫荊樹

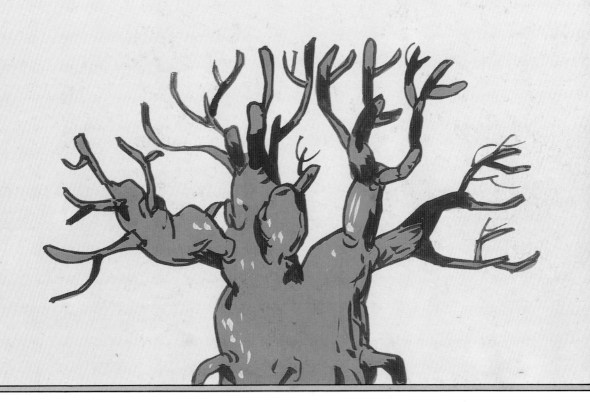

Long ago, there was a farming family of three brothers. Each of the three had a special talent. The oldest was the smartest; he was the accountant of the family. The second brother was the strongest; his work was to cultivate the fields. As for the third brother, he was the most talented in taking care of animals. So, all the cows and pigs of the family were raised by him, and all were indeed very healthy.

從前，有一戶農家，住著三兄弟。這三兄弟各有本領：老大腦筋最好，便負責管帳；老二身體結實，就專門管種田；老三呢，他最會照料牲畜，所以，家裡的牛啊豬呀，全讓他養得肥肥壯壯的。

三兄弟相親相愛的生活在一起，每天傍晚，當他們忙完工作以後，便坐在院子的紫荊樹下喝茶、聊天，談談一些有趣的事情，真是快樂極了！

　　由於三兄弟分工合作，互相幫助，使田裡的收成越來越好，家產便越來越多。

　　鄰居王大頭看見三兄弟這麼和睦，而且錢越來越多，心裡十分嫉妒，就使壞心眼，想讓他們兄弟分家。

The three brothers lived together in harmony. At dusk, after they had finished their work, the three would sit in their yard under the redbud tree to drink tea and chat. They would chat about interesting things. Were they happy then!

Because the three brothers divided the work among themselves and helped out each other whenever needed, the harvest from the fields were more and more plentiful. Naturally, their family's wealth increased.

Their neighbor Busybody Wang saw that the three brothers not only had a great relationship among themselves, but they also were earning more and more money. Busybody Wang became rather jealous of them. So, he thought up a scheme to make the three brothers divide up their property.

Consequently, early the next morning, Busybody Wang ran to the oldest brother who was the accountant and said, "Everyday you have to work so hard in bookkeeping. Why don't you have your own business?"

Next, Busybody Wang ran to the fields and said to the second brother, "Look at you with sweat covering your face while your brother's at home in the shade. It isn't fair at all. Shouldn't you claim your share of the wealth?"

Noticing the facial expressions of the first and the second brothers, Busybody Wang knew that his plan was taking effect. He hurried toward the pigpen to look for the third brother. Busybody Wang said to him, "Everyday, you feed the pigs and cows, getting yourself so dirty and smelly. You must be very frustrated. Why don't you move away and work for yourself?"

　　於是，第二天一早，王大頭就跑去對管帳的老大說：「你每天算這麼多帳，真是太辛苦了！你們為什麼不分家呢？」

　　接著，王大頭又跑到田裡，對老二說：「瞧你累得滿頭大汗，你的兄弟卻在家涼快，真是太不公平了，你們為什麼不分家呢？」

　　王大頭看老大、老二的神情，知道他的話有點效果了，連忙又去豬圈旁找老三，對他說：「你每天養豬、餵牛，弄得全身又髒又臭，真是太委屈了，你們為什麼不分家呢？」

三兄弟被王大頭一說，心裡都很生氣，便吵著要分家。於是，當天晚上，他們就把家裡的財產全部平均分配了。最後，剩下院子裡的那棵紫荊樹，他們決定第二天早上再把樹平分了。

Because of Busybody Wang's meddling, the three brothers became furious and started to argue with each other about the division of their property. As a result, they distributed their property among themselves equally that night. In the end, only the redbud tree was left in the yard. The three brothers decided to split the tree the next morning.

But the next morning, when the three brothers went into the yard, they discovered that their normally leafy tree had suddenly lost all its foliage in a single night. Only the barren branches were left. Soon the redbud tree was going to die!

The three brothers were very startled at the sight! The third brother said, "Wasn't it fine yesterday?"

The second brother said, "Yeah! Why would it change like this?"

The oldest brother said, "Could it be because we are separating from each other and dividing up our property? Could this have upset the redbud tree, making it dry up and die?"

可是，第二天一早，三兄弟來到院子裡，發現那棵長得十分茂盛的紫荊樹，竟然在一夜之間，葉子全掉光了！剩下光禿禿的樹枝，眼看著就要枯死了！

三兄弟看見這種情形，心裡驚訝極了！老三說：昨天不是還好好的嗎？

老二說：是啊！怎麼會這樣！

老大說：難道是因為我們要分家，害得紫荊樹傷心得枯死了！

The three brothers were touched by the redbud tree's sorrowful state. They also grew sad and regretted what they had done. So, they decided neither to leave each other nor to chop down the tree!

No one knew why, but after the three brothers decided not to separate from each other, the redbud tree came back to life. New leaves sprouted from the branches, and beautiful little flowers appeared. The three brothers were so happy that they said, "The redbud tree has reminded us to respect and love each other, and never part company." Ever since then, as they had done earlier, the three brothers lived together happily ever after.

三兄弟看見紫荊樹可憐的樣子，心裡十分難過，也十分後悔，所以決定不分家，也不砍樹了！

說也奇怪，當三兄弟決定不分家以後，那棵紫荊樹竟然又活了過來，樹枝上立刻長出嫩葉，開出美麗的小紫花。三兄弟高興極了，他們說：紫荊樹提醒我們要相親相愛，永不分開。從此以後，他們三兄弟又和從前一樣，過著快樂的生活。

Sibling rivalry is part of children's normal development. Parents need not be overly concerned about rivalry unless there is threat of physical danger. Parents should be mediators, guiding their children toward reconciliation. However, instead of merely telling them not to fight, it is much better to show the benefits of having a cooperative relationship. For example, telling youngsters the redbud tree's story may lead them to an understanding of the blessing of having siblings. If children learn to love their brothers and sisters at home, they will learn to be considerate in relationships outside the family.

Lazy Bones & the Magical Bowl

懶鬼兒和聚寶盆

Long ago, there was a child called Little Po. His father was known to everyone as "Lazy Bones" because he was incredibly lazy. Lazy Bones didn't chop any firewood or fetch any water. He would eat and sleep, and sleep and eat. He used up all the family's money for food. Finally, there was not a grain of rice left in the storage bin. Since there wasn't any other alternative, Mother asked Little Po to go pick fruit from the hillside orchards.

Little Po went up a hill and picked lots of fruit. However, he forgot to take along a basket.

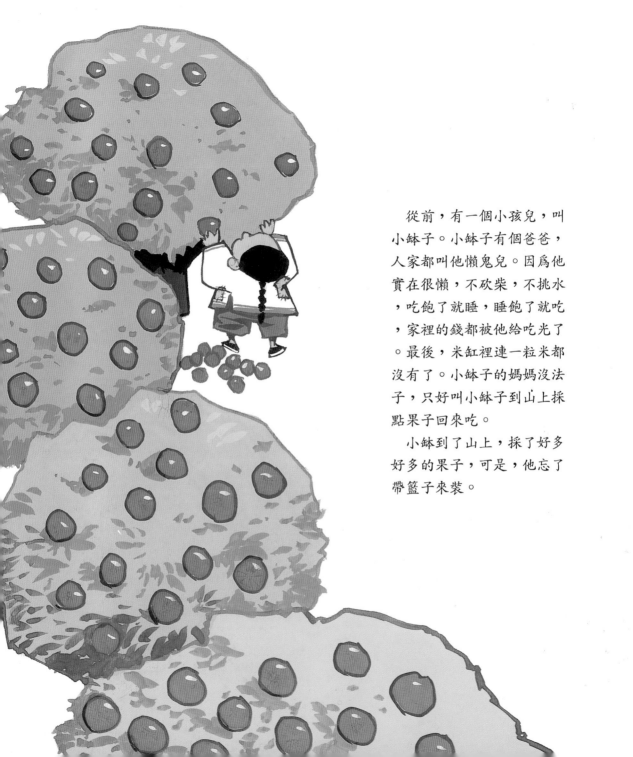

從前，有一個小孩兒，叫小缽子。小缽子有個爸爸，人家都叫他懶鬼兒。因為他實在很懶，不砍柴，不挑水，吃飽了就睡，睡飽了就吃，家裡的錢都被他給吃光了。最後，米缸裡連一粒米都沒有了。小缽子的媽媽沒法子，只好叫小缽子到山上採點果子回來吃。

小缽到了山上，採了好多好多的果子，可是，他忘了帶籃子來裝。

15

While Little Po was puzzling over how to carry the fruit, something suddenly caught his eye. In front of him, on the ground, he saw a black earthen basin. It was just perfect for carrying the fruit. Delighted, Little Po put the fruit into the basin and carried everything home. Papa Lazy Bones saw the basin full of plump fruit and opened his mouth wide. All at once, he ate five, if not six pieces of fruit. Checking the basin, Little Po cried out, "Wow! Didn't daddy just eat five or six pieces of fruit? Why is it still full of fruit?"

Little Po's mother also thought it odd, so she took five more pieces of fruit out of the basin. Again and again she took fruit out, yet there was still a basin full of fruit.

正當他在發愁，突然兩眼一亮，看到前面地上，躺著一個黑不溜俅的瓦盆，正好可以拿來裝果子。小缽子喜孜孜的，裝了果子，抱著瓦盆回家。懶鬼兒爸爸看到一盆子胖咚咚的果子，張開嘴巴，一吃五、六個。小缽子叫了起來：「哇！爸爸不是吃掉五、六個了嗎？果子怎麼還是滿滿的一盆子呢？」

小缽子的媽媽也覺得奇怪，從盆裡再拿出五個果。拿五個，又生出五個，盆裡的果子還是滿的。

"Good heavens! This is a treasure! This is the legendary magical bowl!" shouted the mother. Staring with his big, round eyes and stuttering as if his tongue had been tied in a knot, the father cried out, "Little...Po, hurry and go borrow a coin from Uncle Tsue next door!" Little Po, rather than his usual three, took only two steps and quickly brought home the borrowed coin.

Papa Lazy Bones threw the coin into the earthen basin and then took it out.

"You see, there really is another coin in the basin!" exclaimed the mother pointing.

"The earthen basin can produce money for us! We are now rich!" father said, as he jumped with joy. Papa Lazy Bones kept on throwing coins in and taking out more.

　　「天啊！是個寶貝呢！是傳說中的聚寶盆呢！」媽媽叫了起來。爸爸瞪大了眼珠子，舌頭打了結。「小……缽子，快到隔壁向崔大叔借個銅錢來！」小缽子三步當作兩步，很快的借回一個銅錢。

　　懶鬼爸爸把銅錢丟進瓦盆，再把銅錢拿出來。

　　「你們看，盆裡果然還有個銅錢！」媽指著盆。

　　「瓦盆會生出錢！我們發財了！」爸跳了起來。於是，懶鬼兒爸爸拼命的丟錢，拼命的撿錢……

Since the arrival of the magical bowl, Lazy Bones did away with all his chores. Worse yet, he would take money out of the bowl to go drinking and gambling. When drunk, he would hit Little Po. When he lost at gambling, he would punch Little Po's mother with his fists.

One day, Papa Lazy Bones again put some coins into the magical bowl. Little Po's mother saw what her husband had done and quickly snatched away the magical bowl. She yelled, "I will not allow you to go drinking or gambling anymore!" Papa Lazy Bones wanted to snatch away the magical bowl from his wife, but Little Po was protecting his mother. The three pushed and shoved each other. It was chaos!

現在有了寶盆，他更不幹活兒了。更糟的是，他把盆兒變出的錢拿去喝酒、賭博。喝醉了，就打小缽子；賭輸了，就揍小缽子的媽。

　　一天，懶鬼兒爸爸又放了幾個銅錢到寶盆裡。小缽子的媽看見了，一把搶過寶盆。她叫著說：「不准你再去喝酒、賭博了！」懶鬼兒爸爸上前去搶，小缽子護著媽媽。三個人推推擠擠扯成一團。

　　一下子懶鬼兒爸爸被絆在地上，一屁股跌進寶盆，怎麼使勁，也站不起來了！

　　小缽子和媽媽，一個拉手，一個拉腳，把懶鬼兒爸爸拉出寶盆。哪裡知道，拉出一個懶鬼兒，盆裡還坐著一個真的懶鬼兒。小缽子和媽媽用力的拉，拼命的拉，一個、兩個、三個、四個………一共拉出了十個懶鬼兒，滿屋子亂跑。懶鬼兒爸爸坐在盆裡，大叫：「我還在這兒呢！快救我出去啊！」

Soon Papa Lazy Bones fell down on the floor. His rear end landed in the magical bowl. No matter how hard he tried, he couldn't stand up.

Little Po and his mother, one pulling his hands and the other pulling his feet, got Papa Lazy Bones out of the magical bowl. Who would have ever expected that after one Lazy Bones was pulled out, sitting in the bowl, was the real Papa Lazy Bones. Little Po and his mother pulled as hard as they could. One, two, three, four..... Altogether, they pulled out ten Lazy Bones. All of them were running around wildly in the house. But Papa Lazy Bones was still sitting in the bowl, howling, "I'm still here! Hurry and get me out!"

Little Po found a club. He aimed at the magical bowl and smashed it as hard as he could. "Crash!" The magical bowl was shattered into pieces, and the ten Lazy Bones disappeared into thin air. Papa Lazy Bones had sweat running down his forehead; it took him a lot of effort to stand up.

小缽子找來一根棒槌，對準寶盆用力一敲。「框！」的一聲，寶盆破了，十個懶鬼兒不見了。真的懶鬼兒滿頭汗水，好不容易站起來。

他擁著小缽子，鬆了口氣，說：「寶盆破了，懶鬼兒爸爸也醒了。今天以後，爸爸再也不去喝酒、賭博，要好好的到田裡耕種，到山裡砍柴，賺好多的錢，讓你們有飯吃、有衣穿，過著幸福快樂的日子。」小缽子的媽聽了以後，歡喜的掉下眼淚。

小缽子高興的大叫：「爸爸萬歲！媽媽萬歲！」

Papa hugged Little Po. Sighing with relief, he said, "The magical bowl is broken. Papa finally has awaked. From now on, I'll never go drinking or gambling again. I'll work in the fields and collect firewood from the hills. I'll earn an income to provide food for you to eat and clothes for you to wear. Then we can live as a happy family." Hearing this, tears of joy rolled down Mother's cheeks.

Little Po shouted loudly and joyfully, "Hurray, for Papa! Hurray, for Mama!"

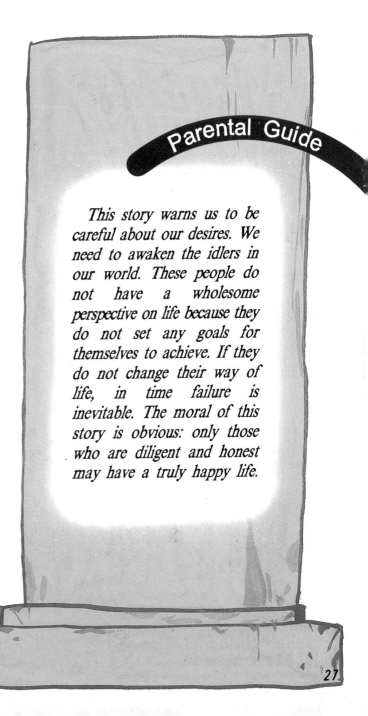

Parental Guide

This story warns us to be careful about our desires. We need to awaken the idlers in our world. These people do not have a wholesome perspective on life because they do not set any goals for themselves to achieve. If they do not change their way of life, in time failure is inevitable. The moral of this story is obvious: only those who are diligent and honest may have a truly happy life.

Chinese Children's Stories **series** consists of 100 volumes; 20 titles of subjects grouped in 5-book sets.

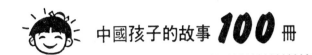

中國孩子的故事 **100** 冊

第 1 ～ 5 冊	中國民間故事	第 51 ～ 55 冊	孝順的故事
第 6 ～ 10 冊	植物的故事	第 56 ～ 60 冊	中國奇童故事
第 11 ～ 15 冊	動物的故事	第 61 ～ 65 冊	中國神話故事
第 16 ～ 20 冊	中國寓言故事	第 66 ～ 70 冊	中國文學故事
第 21 ～ 25 冊	中國成語故事	第 71 ～ 75 冊	中國名著故事
第 26 ～ 30 冊	節令的故事	第 76 ～ 80 冊	中國名人故事
第 31 ～ 35 冊	食物的故事	第 81 ～ 85 冊	中國歷史故事
第 36 ～ 40 冊	發明的故事	第 86 ～ 90 冊	中國地名故事
第 41 ～ 45 冊	十二生肖的故事	第 91 ～ 95 冊	臺灣地名故事
第 46 ～ 50 冊	中國神仙故事	第 96 ～ 100 冊	臺灣民間故事

First edition for the United States
published in 1991 by Wonder Kids Publications
Copyright © Emily Ching and Ko-Shee Ching 1991
Edited by Emily Ching, Ko-Shee Ching, and Dr. Theresa Austin
Chinese version first published 1988 by
Hwa-I Publishing Co.
Taipei, Taiwan, R.O.C.
All rights reserved.
All inquiries should be addressed to:
Wonder Kids Publications
P.O. Box 3485
Cerritos, CA 90703
International Standard Book No. 1-56162-003-3
Library of Congress Catalog Card No. 90-60791
Printed in Taiwan